Heroes
of the
BIBLE

Heroes of the BIBLE

Noah and God's Promises
Moses and the 10 Plagues
Samson

An ARCH BOOKS Gift Collection

*An Inspirational Press Book
for Children*

First Inspirational Press edition published in 1999.

Inspirational Press
A division of BBS Publishing Corporation
386 Park Avenue South
New York, NY 10016

Inspirational Press is a registered trademark of BBS Publishing Corporation.

Published by arrangement with Concordia Publishing House.

Library of Congress Catalog Card Number: 99-71877

ISBN: 0-88486-262-3

Printed in Mexico.

NOAH and GOD'S
PROMISES

Genesis 6—8
for Children

Written by Gloria A. Truitt
Illustrated by Jules Edler

Noah was a godly man
    Who lived quite long ago;
And you can read about his life
    In Genesis, you know.

Now, Noah's family never strayed
    From God as others had;
Although God loved this family,
    The others made Him sad.

Except for Noah's family,
All people loved their sin;

Though once their hearts were filled with love,
  Now evil ruled within.

So God decided what to do;
    He came up with a plan:
With water He'd destroy all flesh—
    All beasts, all birds, and man.

But Noah, in his faith-filled life,
    Was favored in God's eyes,
So God said, "Noah, I'll save *you*,
    Your *sons* and *all your wives.*"

God said to Noah, "Build an ark,"
Then told him how to do it.
The Lord's instructions were exact,
Right down to the last cubit.

And then the Lord said, "When it's done,
   Please follow My design:
Bring in each animal and bird,
   A pair of every kind."

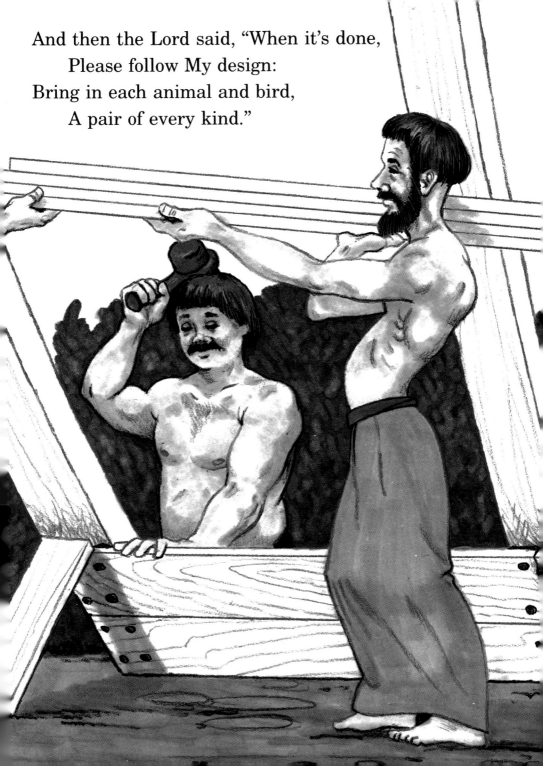

Upon the day the ark was done
The families went inside;
Then came the animals and birds
As God had specified.

Two by two they filed aboard
Before the flooding rain
Would cover every living thing
From mountaintop to plain.

The thunder boomed, the lightning streaked
Through storm clouds thick and dark,
But Noah's family, beasts, and birds
Were snug inside the ark.

The waters filled the valleys deep
And climbed the mountain heights
While Noah's family waited out
Those forty days and nights.

Old Noah was a faithful man.
He knew that by-and-by
The rains would stop and all the land
Would once again be dry.

So when the rains had ended, and
The sun began to shine,
He sent a dove to search the earth
And carry back a sign.

An olive branch proclaimed dry land,
  So Noah's family knew
That they could leave the ark quite soon—
  And all the creatures, too.

Old Noah waited patiently
  Until God spoke the word:
"Go out and take along with you
  Each animal and bird."

Upon a mount called Ararat
  They offered thanks in prayer
To God who saved them from the flood
  With His great loving care.

Now, God was pleased to see the praise
    Of Noah and his crew,
So God announced upon that day
    His promise ever true:

"I'll never bring a flood again
    To cause all flesh to die;
The symbol of My vow will be
    A rainbow in the sky."

Now when the storm clouds gather, and
Big raindrops start to fall,
We do not have to be afraid . . .
God's promise we'll recall.

The sun will shine! God told us so!
And through those shining rays
We'll see His sign, the rainbow, and
To God we'll offer praise.

DEAR PARENTS:

The rainbow is a visible reminder of God's promise never again to destroy the world with a flood. "As long as the earth endures," God said to Noah, "seedtime and harvest, cold and heat, summer and winter, day and night will never cease. . . . Whenever the rainbow appears in the clouds, I will see it and remember the everlasting covenant between God and all living creatures of every kind on the earth" (Gen. 8:22; 9:16 NIV).

God has "remembered" another of His promises, too. It is a promise He first made to Adam and Eve in the Garden (Gen. 3:15) and one He later renewed with Abraham, Isaac, and the family of Israel: "I will bless you; . . . and all peoples on earth will be blessed through you" (Gen 12:2-3 NIV).

The fulfillment of that promise is Jesus Christ, God's Son. Through Noah, God saved the earth from complete desolation; through the death of His own Son, God provided a way of salvation for all from a kind of desolation far worse than any a flood can bring—eternal death and separation from Himself.

Whenever you see a rainbow, remind your child of God's great love for everyone. He loves us so much that He sacrificed His own Son so that we might share eternal life with Him.

THE EDITOR

MOSES *and the* 10 Plagues

Ex. 1:6—12:36 for Children

Written by Connie Hodges
Illustrated by Jules Edler

Long before God's people lived
Within the Promised Land,
They lived in Egypt—welcomed guests
By Pharaoh's command.

But then another Pharaoh
Arose. He was afraid
The Hebrew clans would grow and be
his enemies one day.

"They'll leave my land; they'll leave my rule;
Their loss would be a pity!
I'll turn them into slaves for me
And make them build my cities."

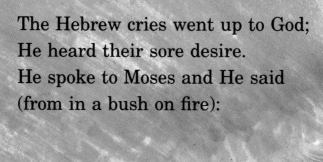

The Hebrew cries went up to God;
He heard their sore desire.
He spoke to Moses and He said
(from in a bush on fire):

"Take these My words to Pharaoh
For he is now My foe:
'I've come to rescue Israel,
So let My people go!' "

"I do not know your Hebrew God,
So, NO!" said Pharaoh.
"Ha! Go and make the bricks we need
And do not be so slow!"

Then Moses did a miracle—
Done by the power of God—
The Nile River turned to blood
When hit with Moses' rod.

The fish all died, the river smelled
As bad as it could be.
But still the heart of Pharaoh
Refused to set them free.

Time went by, but nothing changed.
God's voice was soft and low:
"I'll send the king a plague of frogs
If he won't let you go.

"Frogs and more frogs, tell the king,
Will jump into his home,
In ovens, bowls, and on his bed,
All over will they roam."

But, when the frogs were gone, the heart
Of Pharaoh was ice.
So God sent yet another plague,
This time a plague of lice.

When Pharaoh refused to budge
God sent the fourth plague: Flies—
Flies that flew through everything,
In people's hair and eyes.

The heart of Pharaoh was cold,
He would not lose this battle.
So God sent still another plague:
Black death to Egypt's cattle.

Though this was seen by Pharaoh,
His heart was very slow
To bow to Moses and to God,
To let God's people go.

So Moses gathered ashes up
And spread them in the air.
And when the dust had settled down,
Sores broke out everywhere.

Then God sent hail and fire
And locusts flying low;
But nothing that the Lord would send
Would change this Pharaoh.

Then darkness covered Egypt's land,
So thick it could be felt;
But Pharaoh refused to change
The awful way he dealt.

"The firstborn in the land will die,"
Said God, "That's *every* one.
Tonight the king will feel *this* plague—
He has a firstborn son."

Then Moses told the Hebrew folks,
"It's time to free our race.
Kill lambs and put the blood upon
The doorways of each place.

"Next, roast a lamb and on its meat
Use herbs, and bake some bread.
Stay in your homes till morning comes;
You've nothing, friends, to dread."

Amid the darkest part of night
The angel Death, alone,
Appeared to take the firstborn son
Of each Egyptian home.

When Pharaoh arose to find
His own son, too, had died,
He grieved, "I've lost. And God is God.
Bring Moses to my side.

"Worship God the way you will.
Take flocks and herds along.
Leave this land, soon as you can,
Before we all are gone."

That night they fled from Pharaoh;
Their faith was in their God
Who freed them from their slavery
Through Moses' mighty rod.

DEAR PARENTS

The exciting story of the Exodus from Egypt belongs to Jews and Christians alike. If God had not brought the Hebrews out from their slavery, the entire history of humanity would have been different.

The Lord freed the Hebrews from their oppression both because He was grieved by their suffering and because He was faithful to the promises He had given to them through their ancestors, Abraham, Isaac, and Jacob. God had a special plan for the Hebrew people. Through their history God's saving will and love was to become known to humanity. In Jesus Christ, a son of the Hebrew people, Abraham's family became a blessing to all the earth.

The story of the Exodus is also a story of the power of God over the power of evil. When faced with seemingly insurmountable problems, young children (as well as many adults) wonder if God truly cares about them and is able to help them. The story of the Hebrews in Egypt and their deliverance reminds us that God does not forget His plans for our good, even though after 430 years (Ex. 12:40) it may have seemed so to the Hebrews. Nor can the greatest power on earth prevent the Almighty One from accomplishing His will.

As you read this story with your children, help them focus on this greatness of God's concern and love for His people, including your children. They are His through Jesus, who delivered them from slavery to sin through His death and resurrection.

THE EDITOR

SAMSON

Judges 13–16 for Children
Written by Loyal Kolbrek and Chris Larson
Illustrated by Glenn Myers

Samson had a secret.
He knew he was to be
A Nazirite—God's servant
To set his people free.

He traveled down to Timnah,
And near a vineyard there,
A lion strong attacked him.
Its roaring filled the air.

God's Spirit came to Samson—
No weapon could be found.
He tore apart the lion
And threw it on the ground.

Philistine men caught Samson
With new ropes, tightly bound.
God's Spirit came upon him;
The ropes fell to the ground.

The jawbone of a donkey
Was found nearby, and then,
With this his only weapon,
He killed a thousand men!

Then his enemies waited
At Gaza, by the gate.
They planned to capture Samson;
Their hearts were filled with hate.

But Samson left at midnight.
He left without a sound.
And as he passed the gateposts,
He tore them from the ground.

He put them on his shoulders
And took them miles away.
He left them on a hilltop
Before the light of day.

Samson loved a woman.
Delilah was her name;
And to her home one evening,
Philistine rulers came.

"We'll give you bags of silver,"
They whispered in the night,
"If you learn the secret
Of Samson's power and might."

When Samson came to see her,
She said, "Please tell me true,
How you can kill your enemies,
Without them hurting you?"

"If they use rope," he told her,
"A new rope it must be.
If they bind my hands up tightly,
I cannot break them free."

She bound him; then she shouted,
"Philistine men are here!"
He snapped the ropes off quickly.
The men ran off in fear.

She said, "You say you love me,
Yet mock me with your lies.
Now tell me your great secret,
Dear Samson, strong and wise."

Day after day she teased him,
Until one day he said,
"At no time has a razor
Been used upon my head.

"It was my Lord's commandment
My hair and beard should grow,
And if I use a razor,
My strength will surely go."

One night as mighty Samson
Lay sleeping on the bed,
Delilah called a barber,
Who quickly shaved his head.

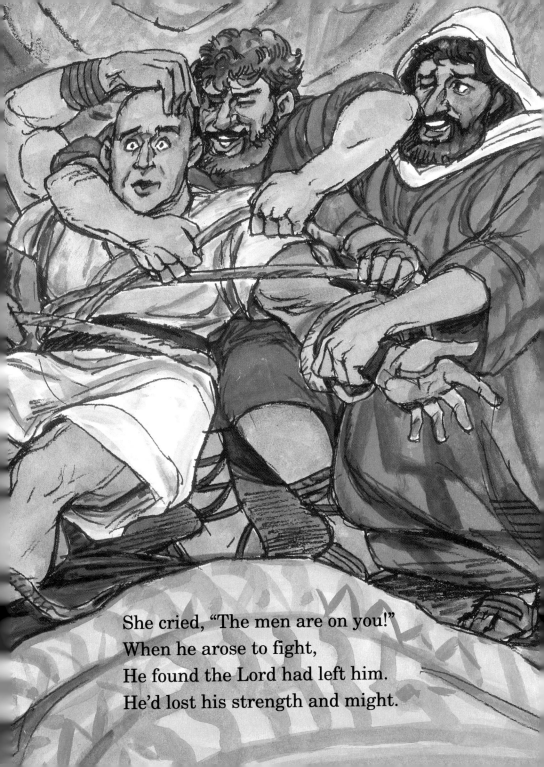

She cried, "The men are on you!"
When he arose to fight,
He found the Lord had left him.
He'd lost his strength and might.

They bound his hands behind him,
Put chains upon his feet.
They blinded him, then led him
Along the Gaza street.

Without God's power to help him,
Bald Samson, weak and blind,
Was shackled to the mill wheel,
The prison wheat to grind.

Day after day he labored,
But people did not know
That as the days were passing,
His hair began to grow.

One day when all were feasting,
Some said, "Bring Samson here.
He'll be our clown to cheer us,
No more a man to fear."

They led him to the temple
Between the pillars high.
He placed his hands upon them,
His face turned to the sky.

He prayed, "O Lord, forgive me
For sinful, selfish ways.
Avenge, dear God, my sightless eyes,
And let me end my days."

The God of Israel heard him
And gave him strength once more.
He pushed the temple pillars.
The roof crashed with a roar.

Three thousand who had gathered
To praise a god of stone,
Fell dead along with Samson.
His work for God was done.

Dear Parents:

At a time when the Philistines were oppressing Israel, God's angel told Manoah's wife that she would have a son. He would be a Nazirite, a specially dedicated servant of God to deliver His people from the Philistines.

Samson's strength came, not from within himself, but from God's Spirit. When, in a moment of weakness, he revealed that the secret of his strength lay in his uncut hair, his enemies were able to cut it off and capture him.

Samson turned to God and asked Him to use him once again to save His people. With his hair long again and his strength restored, Samson pulled down the heathen temple and killed 3,000 Philistines.

God had a special purpose in life for Samson, just as He has placed you and your child in a special place in life for the purpose of serving Him. Celebrate the fact that the Holy Spirit has led you to believe in Jesus as your Savior. Pray together that you will follow His guiding.

The Editor